Rooftop
thoughts

Table of contents

Falling

In Control

The blade kisses her arm	softly
Her fingers hug her palate	quietly
Red pills streak her gullet	innocently
I'm in control she thinks	incorrectly.

Her life has become a mere array
Of things it commands her to do every day,
The demon that entered her corpse long ago,
And whispers, 'you are in control'!

They see that she's in pain,
Think that she's insane,
Cutting into her veins.

But she assures them that she is
Okay, knowing that tomorrow will
Be a new day.

Too late

Pain, red, blood
Emotions flowing out of fresh
Cuts
Emotions she cannot express
Emotions she won't confess.

Her friends beg her to stop
Her haters call her chop-chop
Strangers stare at her in shock
But no one actually gives a fuck.

No one understands why
She cries with her arms and not her eyes.

They say she's doing it for attention
But that's not her real intention.
She's just trying to relieve the tension
That arises from their incomprehension.

Maybe one day
When they look into her eyes, decayed,
They will realize that it wasn't just a game
Knowing that it is too late.

Weightless

I

120 pounds, she looks in the mirror,
Her thighs kiss each other, she has
To be thinner, only then she'll be
Happy, and that is her goal, smile
In a world, over which she has no control.

II

115 pounds, last week she dumped
Sweets and meat and cheese,
she smiles, pleased,
Finally, there's something she achieved.

III

110 pounds, she reached her goal,
The joy is short lived, she knows
She could do more!

IV

104 pounds, people are starting to comment
On her weight at school, you look good
My dear, what diet did you do?

But when she checks her reflection, she sees
That there is still a lot to improve.
Her Thigh gap is only one inch wide, and
When she looks at her corpse from the side,
Her belly is sticking out, when it should
Actually, be the other way round.

V

98 pounds, the scale is her friend,
They meet every day, making sure that
The other is okay.

The people at school have long turned
Away, she is crazy they say, but she
Knows they're just jealous of the progress
She's made!

VI

93 pounds, her body complains, her
Hair becomes thinner and so do her
Nails, she can hardly stand up, without
The world spinning, but she knows that all those

are signs of her winning.

Not eating has long become
A normal thing, indeed, she stopped
Doing anything! Now the only purpose
Of her life is to be thin!

VII

82 pounds, she lies in bed all day,
They say she needs help, that she has
Been led astray, but she knows she's
Fine, she just needs a bit more time
To lose more weight, before she
Can continue with her live.

IIX

76 pounds, the news reporter reads,
She died while sleeping, her heart
Refusing to continue beating,
Her parents, her siblings, her friends,
They all cry,
and everyone asks
Themselves the question
WHY?

She came again this night

The voices in my head just won't subside,
    You're ugly, one of them screams,
    The other, you should die.

My therapist tells me not to listen,
    It's all in your mind, she says,
    A result of your 'condition'.

My friends tell me not to cry,
    Your life is good, they claim,
    You should be satisfied.

My parents won't even look me in the eyes,
    Why are you like this, they ask,
    Can't you be like every other child?

She came again this night,
    Stretching out her hand,
    Saying that she understands.

I followed her into the light,
    Hoping for a better life
    Not noticing till morning that I had died.

Just be positive

'Just be positive',   I hear his voice in my ear,
If having a great life is so easy,   why am I still here?
In this grave black room,   drinking my own tears,
The barricaded door   having been closed for years.

Sometimes a light beam enters the room,
Filling me with strength and hope and I decide
To try my best at having a wonderful life,
After all, I just have to be positive, right?

But before the sun sinks, I realize that it's
All pretence, for me life isn't the flower meadow
It is for them, it is a fight, and being positive
Won't make me win!

Stars

Another day has gone by
Without her swallowing a single bite.
Everyone shivers at her sight,
Swearing that she will die,
But she ignores their lies.

She knows that soon she'll be so
Light she can fly, finally living
A happy life,
Ana has promised, it'll be alright.

And there she is now, up in the sky,
An eternal light watching over you
At night, her lips not forming the
Awaited smile, because her best
Friend lied.

I want to die

Voices around me are screaming,
Drowning the beeping that cuts
Through the air like the blade
I used to deflate my veins.

Can't my heart just stop beating?

I want to shout, let me die!
Rip my skin apart and show them
How I feel inside, make them see
The pain I can't describe.

I don't want to be alive!

Someone squeezes my hand
'Don't worry everything will be fine'.
I can feel their fast pulse, welled up eyes,
But they can't sense mine.

No one will ever understand why.

Cell

They lock me into a cell,
Say that I'm a danger
To my own happiness,
happiness, I mumble,
the word is a stranger.

A therapist eyes me
seriously, says that there,
is hope, I twist my tongue,
another word I didn't know.

After four months they set me
free, you can do this, they say,
you are strong enough to win
the fight, and sometimes I can't
help thinking that they might be right.

Suicide note

Hi,
I just wanted to say
Goodbye.

Let you know that I'm leaving.
That I'll stop breathing.

I'm sure you don't mind.
I'm sure you'll be fine.

I just couldn't deal with it anymore.
My life
The Pain
The war
That I was fighting
Against my demons
On my arms, my thighs, and inside my core.

And I tried, I tried so hard
To get better,
To love myself,
To just be happy,
To get my life together.

But the demons wouldn't subside.
They would eat up my life
And leave me shattered
No matter what I tried.

So I decided to say goodbye,
Please, don't cry.

Who am I?

When I stare into the mirror, I see a face,
Two arms, two legs, wet eyes staring back,
Through this shell, into my inner self,
That they call my name.

Who is this thing? This changing soul,
Which is at once the centre of my life
And nothing at all.

Today it's friendly, tomorrow aggressive,
Right now, it loves me, but that will change
In a second.

Who am I then if my inner self is never
The same? I don't know, please just call me
By my name.

Rising

You are beautiful!

Hey there, yes you,
you are beautiful!
Before you say anything,
this statement is indisputable!

Your eyes sparkle like charms,
And your smile so warm, has
The power to transform
Every heart, indeed, your
Whole body is a piece of art!

Your feet, your thighs, your
Hands, your nails, believe me,
Are all perfect as they are!

And did I mention your skin,
the finishing touch; the carpet
of cells that protects every
part of the unique body
You live within?

Don't ever tell me "I'm not
Beautiful" again! You might
Not see it, but you are a dream!

21 Reasons to stay alive

Depression lies
Your loved ones smiles
Snowball fights

Pizza nights
Bubble baths
Shooting stars

Good old hugs
Collecting mugs
Crazy socks

A cup of tea
Wonderful memories
Swimming in the sea

Your friends
Walking bare feet in the sand
Making plans

Avocado toast
Reaching goals
Inside jokes

Seeing a rainbow
Finding a precious stone
You are not alone!

The sun will rise

Even after the darkest of nights
The sun will rise
Even after months of rain
The clouds will subside
Even after years of pain
You will be alive.

Believe me there's a light
Behind this mountain of misery.

You say you can't see it,
Can you see the sun at night?

The light is there, I have seen it,
You just have to climb and
Reach the other side
Before you can perceive it,
I believe in you, you can do it!

Stronger

I tell you this
You must not quit!
You have come too far
To now slit your wrists.

I'm not saying that your pain
Will ever cease to exist
Or that when you wake up
tomorrow the pills you swallow
will have erased your sorrow.

But a time will come when
You know it was all worth it.

Don't let the tears and the screams
and the feeling of being drowned
put you down!

You are stronger than this!

Letter to myself

Dear me, if you ever doubt yourself
Read this well!

You are fucking worthy,
A unique piece of art no one can recreate,
Stronger than any hardship you've ever faced,
Gentle and kind in all your ways,
More talented than most people these days.

True, you might not be perfect, you too
Have weaknesses, flaws and defects,
But that doesn't mean you're worthless,
No, it means you're special, precious,
Oh, I am jealous!

Right now, you might not see this,
But don't let this deception affect your feelings,
Keep breathing and one day you'll believe it.

Voices

Why?	Don't let your thoughts take over your mind!
Why am I alive?	Don't let others control your life!
I should die!	It's yours alone, and you are in control!
I am stupid!	Don't submit to their nasty tongue!
I am alone!	Declare war on them and prove them wrong!
A failure!	Resist them with all your power!
Unlovable!	Make them cry even louder!
Worthless!	Trying to lead you in the wrong direction!
Hopeless!	Make them suffer from rejection!

WHY?

WHY do I try so hard
To get through today
If tomorrow will just be the same?

WHY am I still alive
If I would rather
Commit suicide
Than live another day
In this unbearable pain?

WHY?

There must be something
That keeps us breathing,
Something that prevents us
From ending this feeling.

Hold on to this inner force,
This jewel,
That makes you prevail
Over the demons in your brain.

Please, don't lose it!

Ready for it

I just want to be okay,
every day,
Smile because I'm happy
Disguise this feeling that

Not think about committing suicide
Live a normal life,
And not because I try to
Eats me up inside.

And I have tried so many times

To be alright
Talked to people
Taken pills

Fought against the demons in my mind
And still, I'm not 'fine'.

It takes time, they say,
To put the pieces back in place.

To fix the damage that has been made,

But I'm ready for it,

whatever it takes!

Tides

Yesterday I cried and
wanted to say goodbye.
Today I smile, and ask
Myself, why would I ever
Want to die?

My happiness is like the sea.
It dies with the tide
And grows with the flow,
It always comes back
Even when I think it won't.

I don't like having
no control
Over the tides,
But what would life be
without a pinch of
Lemon in your tea?

Thank you

The scars on my body,
The tears I have cried,
The times I tried
committing suicide,
Have all made me grow.

Without these rocks
on my way, I wouldn't be
the person I am today,
a warrior, strong and brave.

Thankful for the hardship
I have faced.

Printed in Great Britain
by Amazon

72688391R00020